SUCCESSFUL PEOPLE KISS FOR SUCCESS

AAKASH WAGHMARE

ISBN 979-888521030-0

This book is for all my brothers and sisters who are working hard to achieve their goals in life.

Contents

FOREWORD

This book is a pioneer in clarifying aspects of life. This book is for taking initiative to all friends who want to make their life goals clearly simple and easy. I am sure this will be the easiest way for all of them to achieve the goal.

PREFACE

At every step, whenever we try to achieve something, there is always something that forces us to believe in "luck". Sometimes even when we think we'll win, something happens in the end when the whole game turns upside down. Even after trying a thousand times, the road to success seems as far away as the moon.

So when we see people who take a lot of time and easily do things we can't do, a question always pops up in our hearts, "Are they lucky?" And the brain answers "yes" to it.

Sometimes we keep going on the basis of "luck". But does it bring us any result, any success? I would not like to say anything about success right now but the result is "we always feel helpless, helpless, helpless and tired" isn't it?

This book is about understanding the things of success, which successful people always use. Successful people attract success like a magnet. The game of success is always the most favorite and easiest for them.

But will we ever know this game and easy way? the answer is yes"

You must be surprised to read the title of the book. But yes, that's right!

Successful people "KISS" for success!

Successful people always do everything very easily. And the truth is, "Success is the easiest thing in this world"

You may have bought this book by looking at the strange title of the book, but believe me, there is nothing like it. This is a simple book written for success.

What does this "KISS" mean = Kip Eat Simple Stupid

The title is taken from the book "Rich Dad Poor Dad" by Robert Kiyosaki. And it's not just a marketing method, but the whole book is based on the "KISS" mentioned above.

In this book, you will find answers to the questions discussed below

1. Is success always an inside game as written in most books?
2. You must have often seen the inner energy in every success book. This is also necessary. But still, why doesn't everyone succeed?
3. The more internal energy you raise, the more people you will please, but will you be able to use that energy for yourself?
4. Is there any way to achieve success more easily like other successful people?
5. Is there any practical way to understand that success is really that easy?

This book depicts the physical aspect of life. This book focuses more on making the road to success physically easier than on increasing the energy in the inner part. It is a roadmap for achieving success. For those who are not able to succeed even after reading all the books, it will be nothing less than a boon.

This book explains the laws of success that turn real-life like magic. This is the rule that is equally important for both good and bad people.

Successful people no matter how hard they try to be successful in their lives, but all always use some of the other important principles in the same way. In this book, you will understand the principles that successful people use.

There are no secrets of the different lives of all the people around the world. Rather, the only easy measures are being told here for all the people. Which from history to the present has remained the same at all times and probably will continue to be so.

The first benefit you will get from reading this book is that practically your life will become the most successful and simple. after reading this book, Whatever hard work you have done till today to get success, it will be lesser than 80% in the future, and if it becomes less than 30%, then still you will be as successful as you think.

The second benefit of this will be that you will become great at everything. The road to success you never imagined will open for you. Everything will become easier for you in real life. The third most important advantage in this is that your success time will be reduced by 50%.

For the first publication of this book, I filled it with simple techniques I found from successful people around the world and divided them into 2 key principles. These 2 essential principles will ease every difficult road in your life that you have rarely imagined and this book will open new avenues of success for you that you have never explored to date.

I am sure that after reading this you will be able to succeed in an even better, easier and faster way and that is my wish. I hope you like it and bring happiness to your life.

Note, this entire book is straight to success and focuses on understanding things straight away. This book is for those who are eager to understand the facts of success and not for intrinsic motivation. Instead of adding additional examples, we have added a few examples just to understand the point and pay more attention to the quality of the content. You'll realize this book is more straightforward until you're ready to learn the easy way to success.

Aakash Waghmare

ACKNOWLEDGEMENTS

This book draws from lessons learned from all the best around the world to build a great infrastructure that will help you ease your way to success

PROLOGUE

This book is full of real-world scenarios with example names, changes in place and time, and there may be some sort of story that is fictional and not related to anything else, and if so, it's just Could be a coincidence. This book does not in any way hurt the personal, moral, religious, social, and political sentiments of any person, society, party, company, or any other person. If it happened, it could be just a coincidence, and it has nothing to do with the publisher and the author.

I

First Principle - Trust

This first and most important principle will not only tell you about trust but also tell you how to trust yourself. I am sure you will start believing in yourself after reading this.

"If you have courage, supreme power will help you"

It is said that the cosmic power opens the way for those who believe in themselves.

We must have heard and read this thing often. But have we ever experienced it in everyday life?

The first principle used by successful people for success is "believe in yourself".

Before doing anything, you need to know can you do it? You will not be able to achieve anything without believing in yourself. Whatever you try to do, you will always push yourself back. And this is a very common process.

Obviously achieving success is "easy", but having faith in yourself is equally important.

Without believing in yourself you cannot move even a step ahead in life. You go to sleep every day thinking that tomorrow morning you will wake up well and start your work. Instead, if you don't sleep in fear of death, you will never be able to live properly in life and will eventually die.

Fear is one such thing in our life that prevents us from believing in ourselves.

Some of the following things can happen to you without believing in yourself.

1. You will keep thinking again and again at every step and success will go a long way.
2. You will always hold yourself back out of fear and success will be just a dream
3. You will never be happy in your life

"The essential and first important secret of any success is "believe in yourself". Faith that will give him courage and reveal the secrets of success."

Abraham Lincoln, who was a common man, decided on the basis of his ideas for his presidential candidacy and won. Suppose if they thought, "I'm a normal person, what can I do?"

According to history, the Wright brothers, who built the world's first motorized aircraft, would have become famous if they did not rely on it before flying? Maybe not.

Similarly, faith sets the first step on the road to success and acts as a shield for you.

Understanding faith

Every human has 2 bodies. One is "outer" which is visible and the other "inner" which is not visible, which we call mind.

We are able to trust both the outer body and the inner body because of the mind. This is my body, how can we say? Because with this our heart and mind are connected.

Whatever we do in everyday life, we are able to do it because we believe in those things. Like walking, eating, talking, fighting, and many more. We believe in ourselves to do all these things.

In the same way, it is also necessary to believe in the inner body i.e. mind. By believing in the external body, we can improve our bodies. And by believing in the inner body we can improve our minds.

The outer body will help us to achieve things physically and the inner body will show us the way to those things.

To put this entire book into action, it is necessary that we learn to trust our minds. So does that mean we don't trust our brains?

97 out of 100 people do not trust their minds and this can be tested by a few things.

Suppose we do not know how to swim in the water. We have what we need to swim in the water that will save us. Now we have explained to the mind that we will not drown. Yet how many people are there who think before jumping into the water? Instead of saying that everything is fine, doubt breaks our trust.

So is it wrong to doubt? No, but when everything is perfect, and you have seen, tested, even after that, if you are thinking narrowly before doing something, then this doubt breaks trust.

How many people are there who check their office bags several times every morning before going to the office? Even after locking the house, there are many people who keep checking whether the lock is installed properly or not.

We know everything, yet we shy away from trusting ourselves. Due to this doubt, gradually we get used to it and every work of ours is not done properly or it starts getting late. This doubt forces us to look at every good thing with suspicion in our minds.

Most people impose doubt in their life, which simply means that doubt has taken over their minds. It spoils our life, spoils the relationship, ruins the family. And we can never achieve anything more than this.

Why do we get doubt?

There is always a reason to doubt the "results" that will give us trouble or misery in the coming future. This trouble or misery creates fear in our minds. This fear is always of many things. Among them, there are 7 main ones as,

1. fear of being alone
2. fear of death
3. fear of losing something
4. fear of not understanding
5. fear of losing life
6. fear of losing
7. Fear of losing honor and fame

Fear always stops anything from moving forward in life. It is something that gives us the taste of defeat without even entering the battlefield.

Your brain is a great weapon

Our brain is a superpower for our body. He controls the whole body. But when you try to do the same thing over and over again (despite being confident), your brain will create an emergency and panic state for the body that indirectly tells you "You're not ready to hit Will address with ".

Result - "You Will Lose"

Remember, doing the same thing despite having faith and preparing for something is different here. "Readiness" and "confidence" are two different things. Preparation simply means that you are preparing yourself for something. After this preparation, when you enter the battlefield, most of the 100 people lose faith in themselves from the very beginning or start remembering their preparations again and again.

For example, a person has already prepared for the final examination of his college. When he goes to the examination hall, he starts missing his preparation. It is absolutely wrong to do so.

Missing your preparation on the battlefield is a sign of weakness once you are prepared physically and mentally. It instills fear in your heart. Instead, start attacking your target, and your mind will automatically do all the essentials.

Suppose you enter the examination hall after complete preparation. Now you have to trust your mind and keep it calm. Instead, if you put it into preparation again, the mind will always forget something. As a result, you will feel scared which will make you forget the remaining studies in your mind.

If you set a target and attack it, then the time from setting the target to attacking is called the golden period.

This is the time when you have to trust your brain. And this is the time when we have false trust in our minds.

Result - "The brain doesn't work to its full potential"

In this golden time, when you feel a little scared, then understand that your faith has been lost. However, we are afraid only when we do not know something. But if we have prepared, we have understood the goal, we have made it precise, then after that your mind does everything, and you can earn accolades just by being a spectator.

Ways to clear doubts

Method 1: Gaining Knowledge

Doubt can be removed only when you have knowledge. The knowledge that helps you master everything. Gaining knowledge about whatever creates doubt in your mind will make you feel better and you will become more and more efficient.

Suppose you have prepared properly for your final examination of college. Now you know that if you write your exam properly then you will have no fear of losing in the exam and you will be able to skill yourself in a better way.

Listen - knowledge here does not mean general knowledge of anything.

Knowledge means gathering complete information about your goal. In this important thing like the history of your target, its current position, its weakness, its strong moves and most importantly how to beat or achieve it.

Remember, the consequences of everything you're going to do here should also be taken into account.

When you have all the information, achieving the goal is as easy as drinking cold water from a vessel kept in your house.

But many times it happens that even after doing all the preparations, you are always surrounded by doubts. And as a result, you fall behind in something.

For this, we have to look another way.

Method 2: Understand the result and be prepared

Again let us take the example of the final examination of the college. Let's say you've studied well, you remember everything, and yet you're full of doubts like "Will you to remember everything at the right time?"

Often this problem occurs in students. This problem drives them to move on and give them defeat in their life.

If you ask me, "I would blame doubt for defeat in everything"

If you don't clear the mind of doubt before doing anything, the result will be what you imagined.

Despite all the preparations, if your mind is full of doubt, even if it is one-thousandth of 1%, clear it immediately. Because one rotten fruit will spoil the whole basket.

It would be perfectly fine to think about the consequences of doing so.

Imagine what would happen if you failed the exam. In the same way, you can think about the consequences of whatever you are doing.

Suppose you have prepared your office bag properly. We always check it once again when we leave the house so that we don't have to come back.

This is the reason why the insects of doubt are born in our minds. Once it is born, we become its slaves forever. This slavery comes out of the office bag and starts controlling us at every step of our life.

The result - what we think turns out to be worse than we think. We forget it and always start blaming external things. We read thousands of success books, start learning everything and still we don't even touch success.

How to Kill the Bugs of Doubt

Once you've got your office bag ready, don't check it again. Guess what will happen at most. Suppose that even after doing all the preparations, if there is anything left then there is no problem. This will not end your life.

You will have to go home once again and there will be some trouble. But because of this, your mind will try to accomplish everything at once. Experience is the mother of knowledge. This will keep your mind calm and you will be advised to complete everything in one preparation with your mind.

Result - Your mind will start doing everything right in a completely calm manner. He now knows the consequences of everything and will always keep himself alert to avoid it.

After this, the worm of doubt will never arise in your mind due to experience and knowledge.

Wisdom will teach you that everything is perfect, and the result will teach you what can happen. With this, it will be completely settled in the mind that you will do any work only once and do it with full dedication.

This will make your path to success easier and you will never go back.

Ways to be successful

Successful people always throw themselves into anything. They don't wait to see what happens next. They cut out the suspicious part of their brain and use the full preparation part instead.

Because successful people have no doubts, they always jump with full preparation, even with full enthusiasm, despite being aware of the consequences. And in the end, they are able to stand on their own again even when they are defeated because they have already understood it.

The worm of doubt can wake up again.

The worm of doubt can give birth to itself even in small matters. For this, it just needs a chemical from the forgetting vein of our brain. It is already in a dead state, just because of the chemicals released from the amnesia, it wakes up and starts flourishing.

To end it, always do everything, whether it is mental or physical, in one go with full preparation. And if there's anything left, guess the outcome in advance.

to fully believe

Having complete trust in your mind will make your mind more powerful. It will help you to be the best. Whatever you do, do it with all your heart. Never show weakness.

Worm supplements

Suppose you are once again skeptical for fear of the consequences, do not repeat it a second time so that the skeptical insects do not get a dose.

It may be okay to have doubts when certain things are such that they can end life, but for things that you may fight over and over again, always go to the end without a doubt. Don't be afraid of it.

Be patient, always keep knowledge at hand and prepare for the result. It is called Plan B, Plan C in today's era.

Summary

Faith always paves the way to success. Trust is made of two things. The first is knowledge and the second is to understand the consequences. Knowledge is something you gather to reach your goal, and the result is something that saves you from nature's play.

Knowledge helps you find easy paths. And the result informs of the dangers and thorns scattered across those roads. Both are essential for life. Understanding both gives us complete confidence in ourselves. With this, we are able to achieve our goal without any fear.

Successful people always believe in themselves by understanding both things. And they always seem to climb the ladder of success.

Success is always easy. There is no rocket science in this. It is as easy as our breathing.

In this lesson, we have looked at the first step or principle on the road to easy success. Without this principle, we would never be able to move forward. So start putting it to work in the little things in life.

Always have faith after preparing everything. Remember experience is the mother of knowledge. You will never learn until you experience it. So always after preparation throw yourself in the goal. This will keep your confidence in your mind.

After preparation goes straight to the goal!

In the next lesson, we'll look at essential information about the goal so that we can actually ease the road to success.

II

Second Principle - Goal

"Focusing on the goal doesn't make it necessary to focus on other things."

Often people focus on their weapon more than their target. They get ready for it, sharpen their weapons, and when it comes time to hit the target, they miss.

In the game of archery in the Mahabharata, the historical saga of India, when Acharya Drona asked Arjuna, "What do you see?" To this Arjun said, "I can only see with the eye." Guru Drona asked again and kept asking until he was satisfied, and each time Arjuna gave only one answer, "I see only the eye?"

What does this reveal? Arjuna (the great historical warrior) did not care whose eye it was, as his target was the "eye" in front. Although that eye was of a fake bird. But still, even Arjuna's concentration was refusing to see the bird.

Whenever we go to hit our goal, instead of focusing on that goal, we start preparing to hit that goal. Although preparation is normal, and only a prepared person can enter the goal. But, when it is time to focus only on the goal, we still keep busy with our preparation.

Let us understand this with a real-life example.

A girl who was in class X spent the whole year only preparing for the final exam. For a year he read and memorized all the books. She was such a smart child that it was impossible to beat her. He was not at all proud of his intelligence. She used to help others whenever she wanted. After a year of preparation, when she gave the final exam and the result was that she failed in 2 subjects.

A smart girl who was an expert in everything, but due to some subjects failed in the final exam. What could be the reason for this?

Abraham Lincoln, America's most famous past president, said, "If I was given the time to attack, I would spend more than 80% of that time sharpening my weapons."

Does this mean that Lincoln wants to say that he just keeps sharpening his ax? No, not at all. Rather, it really means that "Whenever they get time, they will do everything possible keeping in mind the preparations made with their given weapon, so as to eliminate their target in one attack".

That girl did exactly the opposite. During the period of attack when she should have used her weapon, she just kept preparing. However, she could have made her target more precise. But instead, she focused on her preparation and as a result, she failed. One of the reasons for failing the exam is "not having faith in your mind".

Does this mean that we should not practice when we are fully prepared? Yes absolutely.

Everything has its right time. Prepare when it's time to prepare. When it's time to attack, do just that.

When you've done everything right, all you have to do is attack. If you are repeating it again and again despite preparing properly, you will forget something in the mess and you will waste your energy trying to memorize it. As a result, you will forget the rest of your preparation.

Preparation means bringing accuracy to mind. After its arrival, use that preparation properly so that you can make your goal more precise. Trust in mind, he will do very well when it is time to attack.

The second step towards the goal

Frame of mind

When a goal is set, it is necessary to prepare. It consists of three stages.

1. Make Basic Preparation
2. Target Concentration
3. Preparing the Right Goal

1. Make Basic Preparation

Preparation simply means creating a framework in the mind. This framework creates a series of correct and precise actions in our brain so that when the time comes, it works as it should.

This structure can break down due to mistrust. That's why we should always strengthen the mind.

Whenever we ask the mind to make a plan of preparation, it does it at that very moment. After that, our body has to get used to it. It can take about 72 hours for the mind to get used to the framework and it can take about 192 hours for the body to get used to.

Here basic preparation means, why do you need it? Instead of preparing thoroughly for your goal, first, understand why you need it.

For example, you need money or you want to become rich. Then instead of trying to get money, try to understand why you need money, and why you want to get rich.

Maybe your heart can convince you that becoming Aamir will bring you respect and fame among the people. So let me tell you, there are many people in India who have respect and fame, without much money.

Remember - this book is for knowing about your goal and its easy-to-understand way. This book is not at all meant to explain to you the good and bad consequences of those methods. Do all that work with your understanding and affinity.

Understanding the "reason" for achieving our goal always helps us to find an easier path.

For example, if you want to learn to swim in the water, the easiest way is to throw yourself in a swimming pool. Nothing can be easier than this. However, it is equally important to have your guide with you.

Know the real reason for achieving your goal so that you can understand every step towards your goal and achieve it as soon as possible by saving time.

Remember: everything is easy in life, just believe in yourself and do the right thing at the right time.

Note: Here, the basic preparation is something like understanding its need in our lives and why it is important in our life.

If you are not aware of the need for a goal in your life, you will find yourself frustrated with just "one problem" on the way to your goal.

2. Understanding the Right Goal in Life (Goal Concentration)

It is most important to have the right goal in life. It depends on the results you want.

For example, let's say you want to earn money. Your goal is to earn money. You have done all the preparations for that, but do you know when your goal will be accomplished?

It is important to have a goal, but more than that it must have a destination. This means that you must have the right goals.

If earning money is your goal then even 1 rupee coming to you can fulfill your goal otherwise you will never know the end of your goal.

Make your goal precise first. No matter how many goals you make in life, you will not be successful unless you think about the end of that goal.

End of target

The right way to set a goal is to understand its end. Let us understand it with an example.

You have to earn money and that is your goal. You have made all the preparations for this. Now after that it's time to make it precise. Now start thinking about how much money you need.

Let's say you want Rs 1 crore. Now you have the right target. And you know whether your preparation is necessary for 1 crore or not. If your preparation can earn 1 crore rupees then you will understand the whole plan.

Later you will be ready for its result. It doesn't matter whether you win or lose. You just have to believe in your preparation and let it happen the right way.

Having a goal in life is very important, so keep it. After that make necessary preparations. When the preparation is done, then spend the remaining time in making the goal accurate. So that you know where to stop.

When you know where to stop, you always prepare thoroughly. And can stop the wasted effort.

Andrew Carnegie did not aim to become America's richest industrialist in the 18th century. His goal was to create the largest steel industry and sell steel everywhere. This is the reason that despite being America's richest person, his industry continued.

When the target is not accurate, break it into pieces

Sometimes the goal of our life may not be precise. Sometimes the goal is such that it will last a lifetime. This will make us feel that we are chasing after the goal all our life and one day we will stop striving for it.

In this period, we should enjoy it by making small things precise while moving towards the goal so that our heart and mind are fit, healthy, and always ready for the next step.

Even though Andrew Carnegie's goal would be to build the largest steel industry, he made every factory his goal. And upon its completion, he rejoiced and celebrated that goal in his heart. This was the reason why he always felt fresh and great.

If not all successful people saw the end of their great goal, they celebrated its success by breaking it down into smaller pieces and making it precise.

This was the real secret of his success.

Whenever you feel that you are not able to see the end of your goal, always break it into pieces. By breaking down goals into small pieces, we know their end and we can make the right preparations to meet them.

Remember - as important as it is to have a goal in life, it is equally important to have an end for that goal. With this, you will be able to take the right step.

If your dream or goal is to become the richest man in the world, then always be the richest man in your household first. After that of his colony. Then city, taluka, district, state, country and then become the richest man in the world.

With this, you will understand how to become the rich man of the world, and that is how you will be able to change yourself in everything.

Do the right thing at the right time

When you are given time to prepare, always just prepare, and when it comes time to set goals, join them. When it's time to hit the target, forget everything and just focus on the target and start hitting the target. At that time it is foolish to see how we will hit the target.

For example, if you are preparing to pass the exam, all you need to do is read and understand the lessons required to pass. But if you want to score more marks in the exam then your goal will be different and so will your preparation.

Now when you enter the exam hall, there is no need to prepare and repeat the test. Instead, you have to have faith in the mind and hit the target.

3. Preparing the Right Goal

When you know your goal, recognize its true need, and understand its end, everything is clearly visible like stars in a clear sky.

The right preparation for that will now be your next task.

Proper preparation tools

If you want to win a cricket match, what will you prepare for it? Will you just improve yourself or do something else?

I think it is more important to know the goal than to strengthen yourself.

When soldiers leave for battle, they always understand both the weak and strong points of the front forces. They understand how to defend themselves in an unexpected situation or how to attack an enemy leader.

So can't we use this method for our life purpose? If we understand our goal properly then we will know, "How much energy we have to put on our goal".

If your preparation is as precise as all those soldiers, you will always be able to wave the flag of victory.

ꕥ

Summary

It is important to have a goal in life. No matter how big your life goal is, you can achieve it in easy ways. You will not have to suffer much for this.

In this lesson we learned that to move towards the goal it is necessary to have a goal. And even more important is the reason.

"Reason" will always keep your mind motivated so that you can always move towards your goal. If you go for something without reason, then after some time you will find yourself disappointed and stop your step towards that goal.

When you have a goal and you know the reason for achieving that goal, now is the time to know the end point of that goal.

The endpoint of the goal means the place where you will stop. The only truth of life is the end. So first understand the end of your goal. If you know where you want to stay then you will be able to reach that place with full enthusiasm.

If you know where to stop, all the roads leading to the goal will be open to you.

When you understand the end of the goal, it is time to prepare to move towards it.

Preparation means the necessary information about the path we have chosen to achieve the goal, complete knowledge about our goal and all the obstacles in it and the preparation done for it.

Remember - Achieving the goal of achieving success is very easy, you just need to believe in yourself and the right preparation for the right goal.

9 798885 210300

Printed by Libri Plureos GmbH in Hamburg,
Germany